ROYAL
FAILIMAL
SOCIETY

EXTINCT FOR A REASON

A Field Guide to Failimals and Evolosers

Scott Cooney and Aaron Adler

GALLERY BOOKS

New York   London   Toronto   Sydney   New Delhi

Gallery Books
A Division of Simon & Schuster, Inc.
1230 Avenue of the Americas
New York, NY 10020

First Gallery Books trade paperback edition May 2013

GALLERY BOOKS and colophon are registered trademarks of Simon & Schuster, Inc.

For information about special discounts for bulk purchases, please contact Simon & Schuster Special Sales at 1-866-506-1949 or business@simonandschuster.com.

The Simon & Schuster Speakers Bureau can bring authors to your live event. For more information or to book an event contact the Simon & Schuster Speakers Bureau at 1-866-248-3049 or visit our website at www.simonspeakers.com.

Designed by Aaron Adler

Manufactured in China

10   9   8   7   6   5   4   3   2   1

Library of Congress Cataloging-in-Publication Data is on file.

ISBN 978-1-4516-8695-1
ISBN 978-1-4516-8697-5 (ebook)

To Veronica, Anastasia,
Molly, and Charley

Contents

Introduction

It's dawn in the Cenozoic era. The earth is lush and green. Among the birds and mammals roaming the veld are the primordial ancestors of many of the animals we know today. Look up—there's Combover Eagle, surveying the earth from his aerial view! You can see his thin strands of hair blowing in the wind as he searches for food and a nice down-to-earth female who's not too choosy . . . .

And down below is Centichicken, his numerous leg pairs undulating as he pursues a startled stag beetle over a fallen log . . . .

Suddenly the canopy bursts to life! It's Feral Poodle—awakening the ancient forest with his terrifying yelps for sustenance.

Off in the distance, Pleather Cow creaks convincingly across the plains, his oh-so-realistic exterior blending almost effortlessly with the herd.

The fossil record is littered with examples of animal adaptations that eventually fell by the wayside to make room for those more suited to evolution's constantly shifting expectations—of failed organisms that briefly but valiantly spread their misguided wings, lamentable fins, and unfortunate flagellum in a bid to stake out a more secure branch on the genealogical tree. Although some evoke comparisons to more enduring species, others bear little resemblance to their present-day successors.

Yet all these animals, while ultimately weeded out of the evolutionary chain, helped pave the way for the creatures we know and love today. You could fill a book with animal species that came to an abrupt end, bowing to nature's fickle, ever-changing demands. And so we did.

Meticulously researched and with references pulled from a variety of sources, it is the authors' hope that this guide will raise awareness and inspire others to learn more about these unique, luckless creatures.

Before there was Darwin, before there was man's best friend, there were . . . Failimals.

NEOPOLITAN ZEBRA

Flavorus Varietus

In an effort to address perceived boredom with the same old two-toned product, the famously striped grass-eater set himself apart from the herd by separating his two colors and adding a distinctive third to the mix. With a different flavor for each of his three sections, this "something for everyone" approach was initially seen as a distinct courtship advantage, advertising himself as the best of all worlds in one convenient container.

But marketing isn't a black-and-white science, and the tricolor tactic soon turned into a public relations disaster. In spite of his novelty appeal, more sophisticated mates were actually turned off by his pandering attempts to be all things to all equids. Complicating things further, the new offering began to attract a wider diversity of predators, and it wasn't long before the plains were littered with unfinished carcasses, carnivores having dug into their favorite zebra flavor and leaving the other two untouched. By the time natural selection had cleaned up this nearly epidemic health crisis, it had become abundantly clear that some products of evolution are better in theory than they are in practice.

FEEDS ON: *Acceptance, approval, pleasing all of the animals all of the time.*

HABITAT: *Inhabits whatever plain you want him to inhabit.*

DEFENSE MECHANISMS: *Insists he is just trying to be accommodating.*

MATING HABITS: *Is often stood up for being too noncommittal.*

NEOPOLITAN ZEBRA

COMBOVER EAGLE
Harpyopsis Decepticus

Nowadays, most would agree that the bald eagle is one of most dignified creatures ever to grace the back of a dollar bill. But there was a brief moment when Mother Nature went against her better instincts, compensating for an inherited lack of plumage up top by plastering a few wispy feathers laterally across his head in a sad attempt to step up his sex appeal.

Of course, birds of prey are supposed to be above such vanity, and in hindsight the cover-up seemed transparent in every sense of the word. Available hens were too polite to say anything, but it was clear his increasingly ridiculous deception wasn't fooling anyone. Refusing to let down the subterfuge, he continued to fly solo until his feathers simply became too thin to work with, at which point natural selection intervened, taking the genetic fugitive and his follically challenged charade out of the mating game for good.

FEEDS ON: *Takeout and cold leftovers, night after lonely night.*

HABITAT: *Lonely cliffs, lonely seacoasts, lonely trees.*

DEFENSE MECHANISMS: *Denial, self-delusion, refusing to accept heredity.*

MATING HABITS: *Usually goes back to the perch alone.*

COMBOVER EAGLE

MAMA'S JOEY
Eternis Singlus

There comes a point in every marsupial's life when it's time to leave the pouch. But this eternally adolescent macropod decided he just had it too darned good, seeing no reason to part with the free shelter and unlimited meals afforded by his maternal parent's fur-lined spare bedroom.

Of course, it's hard to find meaningful work in the harsh, unforgiving climate of the outback, but even a dry, barren economy couldn't completely account for his lack of ambition, and his creepy closeness to his mother's teat was a red flag to the single females in the herd, who always found coming back to his pad a little awkward. In spite of assurances that he had his (quite large) ears to the ground and should be hearing back about something "any day now," this genetic underachiever ultimately failed to make the leap to maturity.

FEEDS ON: *Milk and whatever else is in the fridge.*

HABITAT: *Rarely ventures outside of the soft, comforting pouch of home.*

DEFENSE MECHANISMS: *See habitat.*

MATING HABITS: *See Latin name.*

MAMA'S JOEY

CENTICHICKEN
Pollus Centipus

You could have knocked scientists over with a feather when they first discovered this flightless freakshow, who, perhaps in response to an inadequacy in the wings department, flipped the bird to his avian roots by producing an extra set of legs . . . over and over and over again. Even in the genetically permissive, "anything goes" environment of the late Paleogene, competitors' mandibles would have hit the jungle floor whenever this cockscombed curiosity made his appearance, with potential foes never failing to do a double (and a triple . . . and a quadruple) take as they stood watching the convoluted clucker's interminable segments scurry on by.

Such a grounded commitment to the terrestrial life had its perks, and the extended egg-layer's ability to scrabble up trees and cliff faces to literally scare up his next meal was certainly nothing to scratch at. But in the end, this earthbound aberration ran afoul of good sense, and with the simultaneous rise of hot-sauce-producing flora and the spread of tasty sides like collard greens, corn, and gravy, the free-range Frankenbird soon became a one-stop shop for predators that came to see his endless leg-thigh-breast combinations as a delicious, affordable dinner for the whole family.

FEEDS ON: *Messing with predators' heads.*

HABITAT: *Seemingly everywhere at once.*

DEFENSE MECHANISMS: *Minimal. Once they swallow his appearance, predators find him talon-licking good.*

MATING HABITS: *Let's just say reproduction involves a lot of scrambling and balancing and weirdness and some very long eggs.*

CENTICHICKEN

GERICURLAMB
Ovis Greasius

There was nothing domesticated about this dyed-in-the-wool hustler, whose dynamite rug of crimped, glistening curls alerted the flock that he was anything but a follower. With his luminous locks and sly meadowsmarts, the ovine operator was always on the prowl, melting the ewes with his silky smooth bleats before taking them back to his pasture for a shag.

While the pimped-out merino certainly got his share of shearling, his conquests eventually developed an immunity to his ultrarelaxed flow, opting for steady husbands who would raise their own lambs right and not stray too far from the fence line. His product-heavy pelt proved more of a curiosity than a long-term advantage, and for all his slick talk, this funky-fleeced player turned out to be full of jive.

FEEDS ON: *Fine females in estrus, wherever they be found.*

HABITAT: *At the end of a trail of thick, slimy residue.*

DEFENSE MECHANISMS: *Usually slips out the back door when things get too serious.*

MATING HABITS: *Always has a few ewes waiting on the side.*

GERICURLAMB

ORTHODOX CARDINAL
Avis Evangelicus

This sanctimonious songbird seemed to answer to a higher mating call, taking it upon himself to enforce a strict moral code on the other citizens of the woodland. Perhaps interpreting his extra-prominent crest as a sign of divine authority, he spent his days consecrating ponds, presiding over hatchings, and making sure copulation didn't occur outside the mating pair.

But while revered by members of his flock, not everyone was so enthused to receive the plumed parson's blessings. Some found it hard to turn the other wing when he stuck his beak into their personal affairs, and his constant refrains for the faithful to regurgitate up their hard-earned earthworms whenever he passed the offering nest got more than a few tail feathers in a twist. Alas, when he tried to convert a particularly agnostic turkey vulture into the fold, he finally achieved permanent martyrdom, and the pious Passeriform was unceremoniously exorcised from the evolutionary program.

HABITAT: *Wherever his flock needs him most.*

DEFENSE MECHANISMS: *Preachiness, moral outrage, bringing the Lord into it.*

MATING HABITS: *Supposedly abstinent, but who knows.*

FEEDS ON: *Omnivorous, but with a labyrinthine set of dietary restrictions regarding insects on certain holidays.*

ORTHODOX CARDINAL

Illustration courtesy of the Center for Failimological Research
Copyright 2013. All rights reserved.

TICKLE RAY

Mantus Gigglius

Anyone who says Mother Nature doesn't have a sense of whimsy need look no further than this thin slice of fun, whose uniquely stimulating appendage had its way with the soft, sensitive underbellies of the aquatic world. During his delightful reign of mirth, this undersea jester had the seafloor in stitches, and a single touch of his titillating tail would send victims convulsing into involuntary bubbles of joy.

But not every reef-dweller was amused by this pelagic provocateur's lowbrow shtick, and after molesting one too many hammerheads having a bad day, his act finally jumped the shark and the laughter came to a particularly gruesome end. While the Piscean prop comic will certainly be missed, perhaps his meaner, stabbier cousin would have been better suited to deflect unwanted pitfalls of Cenozoic celebrity.

FEEDS ON: *Plankton, small fish, the laughter of his peers.*

HABITAT: *A never-ending bubble of mischief.*

DEFENSE MECHANISMS: *Laughably inadequate.*

MATING HABITS: *Monogamous, but with a kinky side.*

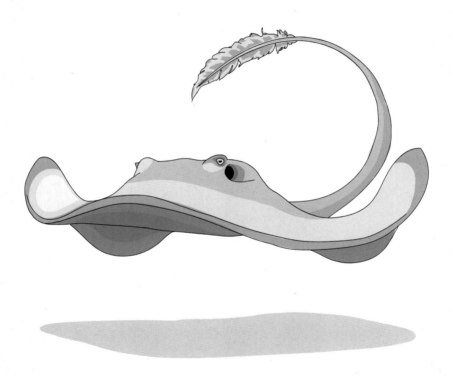

TICKLE RAY

Illustration courtesy of the Faildubon Society
Copyright 2013. All rights reserved.

INFORMAL PENGUIN
Spheniscus Casualis

When you live and mate on an exclusive, hard-to-find landmass where the nightlife generally carries on for a third of the year, chances are you want to look your best. But this buoyant bohemian refused to stand on ceremony, ditching the formal black-and-white attire of his sophisticated peers in favor of looser, more casual patterning. Claiming the stuffy appearance of his forebears was totally Paleozoic and that it was what was under one's waterproof down that truly mattered, the subpolar slacker's relaxed approach to ice-cap living created a more chilled-out social environment where one could kick back, have a few krills, and maybe get a clutch or two incubated on the side.

But sliding on an epoch-old tradition is a slippery berg, and the tendency to push the boundaries of appropriateness eventually caused a flap. The slipshod squid-eaters began showing up to fjord functions in little more than their wooly underfeathers or skimpy coverings that practically put their subcutaneous layer of fat on display for the whole rookery to see. And while a dress code was never carved into the subglacial bedrock, more dignified waddlers found it hard not to look down their bills at this slovenly seabird, whose presentation hardly seemed befitting of a family capable of tracing its lineage back some 30 million-odd years. Frozen out of the better breeding opportunities, the flightless philistine continued to hang out on the periphery of the huddle, but while waiting for an RSVP to mingle his scruffy genes, his official invitation must have ultimately gotten lost in the shuffle.

FEEDS ON: *Likes to nosh, rarely makes a big production of mealtime.*

HABITAT: *Frequently drops by friends' nest sites unannounced.*

DEFENSE MECHANISMS: *Insists he gets his work done just as well as anyone else, so just chill out, man.*

MATING HABITS: *Enjoys the occasional casual bond, but doesn't like to put a label on things.*

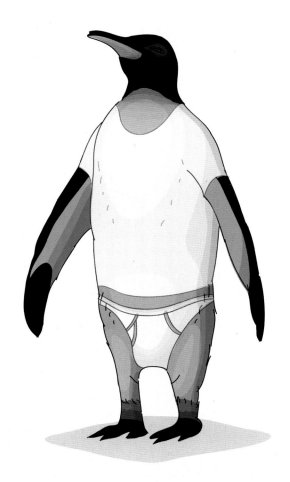

INFORMAL PENGUIN

Illustration courtesy of the Failimal Literacy Project
Copyright 2013. All rights reserved.

GOTH SLOTH
Xenartha Morbidicus

Already having made a name for himself as the most lethargic herbivore in the forest, this morbid tree-dweller took his trademark apathy to a sullen extreme. With his gloomy black fur and pale complexion, Goth Sloth intentionally alienated himself from his peers, rarely coming down from his branch and preferring to hang upside down endlessly like a melancholy pendulum of isolation and despair. To him, the act of foraging for tender shoots seemed an exercise in pointlessness, and he would sometimes use razor-sharp twigs to cut on his furry wrists as an act of revenge against a universe that just didn't care.

Needless to say, these macabre tendencies did not bode well for the creature in the long run. He was generally unprepared or uninterested in the demands of adulthood, and while attracted to others with a similar aesthetic, he tended toward abstinence rather than risk introducing a new life to suffer the cruel indignities of such a vapid and meaningless existence.

FEEDS ON: *What's the point of feeding when we're all careening toward the same inevitable end?*

HABITAT: *Mundane branches, insipid vines, meaningless boughs.*

DEFENSE MECHANISMS: *Apathy, self-mutilation, whatever.*

MATING HABITS: *Please, that is so banal.*

GOTH SLOTH

PEANUT-ALLERGY ELEPHANT

Pachydermus Fuckedicus

Life was hard enough growing up in a land riddled with recurring drought, calf-stealing lions, and the occasional hominid that wants to see your teeth made into an opium pipe. But when his favorite food became off-limits, that was all this legume-loving land mammal could bear. Asthmatic reactions don't play well when you're trying to intimidate a hungry wildcat, and all those hives are tough to itch when your only scratcher is itself swollen with eczema.

From time to time he would attempt to lay off his salty Achilles' heel, hoping nature would forget about his sensitivity to the protein-packed treat. But in the end this wheezing shell-cracker succumbed to his biology, and the irresistible siren call of the groundnut he loved so much was the final straw that broke the pachyderm's back.

FEEDS ON: *Trunkfuls of antibiotics.*

HABITAT: *Wherever he isn't reminded of that terrible, wonderful bean.*

DEFENSE MECHANISMS: *Unsightly hives, projectile sneezing.*

MATING HABITS: *Potential mates give him a chance, but he always turns the conversation back to his allergies.*

PEANUT-ALLERGY ELEPHANT

Illustration courtesy of the Institute of Applied Failimal Science
Copyright 2013. All rights reserved.

CANKLE FLAMINGO

Anklus Corpulus

Considering the way her clunky calves merged with her husky white ankles and plump webbed feet, you'd think this unwieldy wader would have made a bigger splash in the evolutionary pond. Scientists theorize her stocky lower limbs might have provided an advantage in cooler waters, but that seems to be where the benefits of such graceless gams ended.

In spite of a down-to-earth personality, suitors were scarce, flight was a no-go, and even a blind prawn could hear her husky hocks splashing around indelicately from a mile away.

As time went on, the figure-challenged filter-feeder increasingly confined herself to flattering reeds and long, concealing grasses, rather than subject her thunderous trunks to the ridicule of her twiggier cousins. But while fossil evidence is incongruously slim, it's heartbreaking that this one never got off the ground.

FEEDS ON: *Whatever she can smash with her big fat cankles.*

HABITAT: *Extremely firm-bottomed lakes and estuaries.*

DEFENSE MECHANISMS: *Swears she'll hit the gym before the breeding season begins.*

MATING HABITS: *Surprisingly picky.*

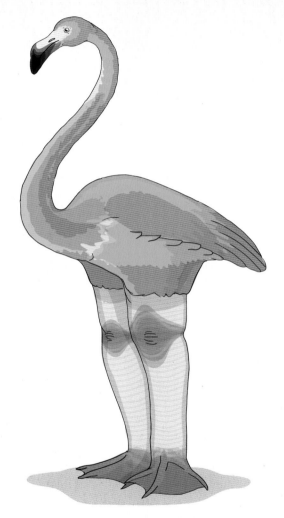

CANKLE FLAMINGO

BONO-BO
Chimpus Insufferablus

In the entire history of advanced primates, it's hard to find one who took their evolved status more seriously than this high-profile ape, who used his fame and lofty standing within the simian community to weigh in on whatever political issue came across his branch. Be it papaya conservation or equal rights for gibbons, Bono-bo swung onto the scene, ready to take up the mantle as self-proclaimed spokeschimp for the latest cause du jour.

But in spite of his altruistic agenda, some apes were turned off by his ubiquitous public presence. And while his intentions seemed admirable, his overbearing persona, which swung between the slightly pompous and the near-messianic, often overshadowed the very issue he was trying to call attention to. In the end, it seemed the majority of the community resented him for exploiting his status as a rain forest celebrity. Although, the more he talked, the more everyone realized that no one could really remember what he did to become famous in the first place.

FEEDS ON: *Publicity, media attention, his own bullshit.*

HABITAT: *Highly visible tree branches.*

MATING HABITS: *Comes off as giving, but always ends up being all about him.*

DEFENSE MECHANISMS: *Insisting it isn't all about him.*

BONO-BO

BURNT UMBERJAY

Crayolus Obscurus

Before landing on the popular indigo version we know today, nature at one point decided to get creative, rounding out the avian spectrum with a rainbow of less primary-colored shades. Perhaps one of the more enigmatic of these was Burnt Umberjay. Not quite tan, not really mahogany, this mysterious bird became something of a cult favorite, with his obscure tint of plumage and a taxonomy that begged the question, "What exactly is an umber, and why would anyone want to burn one anyway?"

But while he must have held some novelty appeal, the woods seemed to be on a different wavelength, and the oddly hued corvid found himself being selected from nature's box of colors less and less frequently. Eventually he was driven out by his bolder, more cerulean cousin, as evolution decided to play it safe and color between the lines. Like his friends Maroon-Breasted Robin, Aquamarine Grouse, and Periwinkle Owl, this off-color subspecies failed to make the evolutionary palette, and today he lives on only in the 64-color variety pack of collective forest memory.

FEEDS ON: *Lemon-Limes, Yellow-Oranges, Cornflowers, Maize.*

HABITAT: *Goldenrod meadows, Pine Green trees.*

DEFENSE MECHANISMS: *Hiding between the Orchids and the Thistle.*

MATING HABITS: *Intimate relationships are often Bittersweet.*

BURNT UMBERJAY

Illustration courtesy of the Museum of Failular Zoology

KOALAMPREY
Adorablus Ohshiticus

What do you get when you cross one of the outback's cuddliest leaf-eaters with the most hell-spawned perversion of nature ever to terrorize God's green earth? It might look something like Koalamprey, who used his plush, stuffed animal-like appearance to nuzzle up to victims before attaching his rows of horny teeth and probing, rasplike tongue to gorge on the life-giving fluids within.

Young joeys spent their first six months lovingly suckled by their mother's milk, at which point the precious demonseed would bore through her pouch in search of his first unholy bloodmeal. Feeding on whatever he could get his button-cute paws on, the irresistible pox on all things holy terrorized both koalas and nonkoalas alike, as mistaken partners would often approach from behind, expecting to snuggle with their fuzzy mate only to be confronted with an endless gaping maw of flesh-lacerating horror.

Mercifully, his food supply was depleted when almost all the species in the immediate subcontinent fled in panic. Turning on one another in a stomach-churning nightmare of cannibalistic perversion, the adorable threat to the very balance of good and evil in the universe finally extinguished himself, at which point scientists hypothesize that his soul was sent back to the noxious, stench-ridden realm of Hades from whence it was conceived.

FEEDS ON: *Soft tissue, bodily fluids, God turning a blind eye.*

HABITAT: *Eucalyptus forests, gum tree coppices, the frozen lower circles of hell.*

DEFENSE MECHANISMS: *His snuggly little paws, his fuzzy wuzzy little ears.*

MATING HABITS: *Far too gross to go into.*

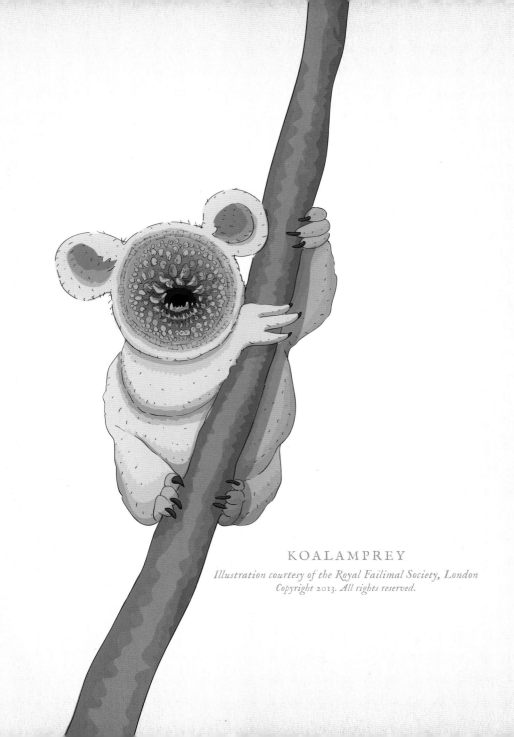

KOALAMPREY

Illustration courtesy of the Royal Failimal Society, London
Copyright 2013. All rights reserved.

BUNNY SLIPPER

Lepus Mocassus

Softer and fluffier than the ubiquitous hoppers we know today, these ancient variants came lined with an irresistibly soft coat of fur both outside and in, to ensure their survival during the long Cenozoic winters. Steadfastly monogamous, they rarely strayed far from their mates, who usually came in identical sizes and often looked so similar it almost appeared as if they were made just for each other.

Tragically, their plush, cushy bodies proved attractive to more than just potential mates; prehistoric beasts discovered that by stepping into them they could keep their cold-blooded feet toasty and dry, and when the Ice Age hit, everybody had to have a pair. It wasn't long before every hominid, tetrapod, and brachiosaur was extolling the comfortable virtues of these floppy-eared foot-warmers, and, before you knew it, even the irregular sizes were all out of stock.

FEEDS ON: *Soft fruits, plushy grasses.*

HABITAT: *Popular in drafty climates.*

DEFENSE MECHANISMS: *Predators often lose interest if one mate disappears.*

MATING HABITS: *Almost always pairs for life.*

BUNNY SLIPPER

OVERCOMPENSATING SHRIMP

Runtus Rippedicus

When your name is shorthand for a pronounced lack of stature, sometimes you have to do something to give yourself a leg up. This diminutive crustacean gave himself all ten, working his limb pairings until they were as pumped and rippling as the sea is briny.

But this newfound buffness may have gone to his head section. A volatile cocktail of brawn and insecurity, an increasing vein of aggression soon had him trolling the seafloor looking to "accidentally" scrape shells with less conflict-inclined ocean life, and when he finally picked on the wrong prawn, the pugilistic decapod found himself in over his antennae. His oversize opponent promptly gave him a well-deserved pounding into the sand, and, in the grand scheme of nature, this jumbo-size shrimp scampi quickly turned out to be little more than an evolutionary oxymoron.

FEEDS ON: *Plankton powder, algae shakes, exaggerated machismo.*

HABITAT: *At the reef, lifting heavy shells and corals.*

DEFENSE MECHANISMS: *Loud talking, aggressively flexing his swimmerets, puffing out his carapace to make himself look bigger.*

MATING HABITS: *Some things can't be enlarged no matter how hard you work at it.*

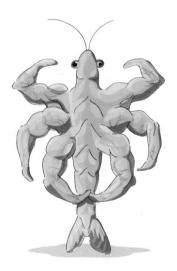

OVERCOMPENSATING SHRIMP

Illustration courtesy of the Center for Failimological Research
Copyright 2013. All rights reserved.

BUCKTOOTH SWAN

Cygnus Dorkyus

When you come from a species known for quiet dignity and restraint, your slightest imperfection tends to be magnified. But this awkward cygnet's conspicuous overbite seemed to underscore an even larger flaw, and his lack of social graces had the flock dipping their necks underwater whenever he swam near. His nasal, lisping honk could be heard from several fens over, and his spastic flapping sent ripples throughout the tranquil wetlands surfaces. Known to splash right up and ask indelicate questions about which swamp one came from, or one's favorite kind of pond grass, he often did so with a generous plug of algae stuck between his unfortunate choppers.

Even so, his family refused to turn their rumps on this witless waterfowl, persistently attempting to include him at marsh functions. But whenever he would tactlessly break conversation to waddle ashore and loudly greet whatever hungry crocodile or ill-tempered wolverine was strolling nearby, each parent could do little more than hiss their disapproval and blame the other's side of the lake.

FEEDS ON: *Uncomfortable silences, inappropriate questions, situations where he is likely to screw something up.*

HABITAT: *Whichever pond he is wanted in least.*

DEFENSE MECHANISMS: *A total lack of self-awareness.*

MATING HABITS: *Awkward around both sexes.*

BUCKTOOTH SWAN

Illustration courtesy of the National Failimal Conservatory

WAIF WALRUS
Odobenus Anorexicus

As body types go, walrus figures have always tended towards the, shall we say, "Rubenesque." But as the species *Odobenus rosmarus* emerged spectacularly from the Ice Age, a new breed began to turn heads in the pinniped world. Forgoing bulk and fortitude in favor of a more slimmed-down silhouette, this svelte bachelorette had the bulls barking and the cows gnashing their tusks as even attached males wooed her with the finest sea cucumbers and bivalve mollusks the Arctic Circle could offer.

But even before the jealous females launched a plan to torpedo this underweight home-wrecker, she ended up doing herself in. Formerly "lucky" mates were quickly turned off by her high-maintenance attitude and constant complaints about being chilly. And when she finally hinted in a not-so-subtle manner that they should lose a few pounds themselves, the skinny bitch finally found herself hung up on the ice shelf for good.

FEEDS ON: *Algae salad, some kelp, a bite of mollusk, occasionally. Really though, it's okay, she's not all that hungry.*

HABITAT: *On thin ice with the other cows.*

DEFENSE MECHANISMS: *Comparing herself to heavier females.*

MATING HABITS: *Puts her best flipper forward, but quickly becomes a pain in the blubber.*

WAIF WALRUS

PLEATHER COW
Bovus Inauthenticus

In a short-lived attempt to trim some fat from the budget, evolution introduced this faux-skinned heifer to the range as a cheaper alternative to the traditional steer. Lightweight and easy to clean, his synthetic hide was cheaper than the real thing, and as the cattle population was beginning to explode, this low-maintenance imitation seemed a sensible way to cut down on materials costs.

But clothes make the steer, and the brand-conscious herd was quick to spot the cheap knockoff, whose inferior hide was considerably creakier and less breathable than the genuine article. As such, cows refused to date such an obvious imposter, and the rest of the herd soon called bull as this bogus bovine was quickly put out to pasture.

FEEDS ON: *Artificial plants.*

HABITAT: *Fake pastures, fraudulent fields, inauthentic meadows.*

DEFENSE MECHANISMS: *Deception, artifice, duplicity.*

MATING HABITS: *Makes a decent enough first impression.*

PLEATHER COW

Illustration courtesy of the Failimal Literacy Project
Copyright 2013. All rights reserved.

CHAUVINIST PIG
Swinus Misogynous

For one of the smartest domesticated animals, this sexist swine's views were hopelessly stuck in the mud. Bristling at the idea that a sow's place was anywhere but raising piglets, the macho hog insisted on being waited hand and hoof around the pen by his mate, even as he grunted and complained that her hocks were getting fatty. On weekends he hung out with the other sausages late into the night, commenting on the udders of finer squealers or even porking one behind the old ham's back, all the while claiming he was busy out "bringing home the bacon."

Studies suggest his bigotry may have come from leftover resentment of a mother who weaned him too early, though he would be quick to dismiss this as a load of tripe. While vestigial traces of his outmoded attitude can still be found today, as liberal views on gender become increasingly common in the barnyard, his opinions are regarded as more and more unkosher, and today he is generally considered to be something of a boar.

FEEDS ON: *Secret, deep-seated feelings of inferiority.*

HABITAT: *At home complaining about the slop, or out drinking with the hogs.*

DEFENSE MECHANISMS: *Insisting the damned sow drove him to it.*

MATING HABITS: *Engages in macho displays designed to attract females with low self-esteem.*

CHAUVINIST PIG

Illustration courtesy of the Faildubon Society

MAID-MER

Sirenus Tragicus

Tales of half-fish, half-human temptresses have seduced seafarers since time immemorial. In this case, the sea couldn't have gotten it more wrong, regurgitating up a cruel hoax of marine biology by taking a pleasing posterior and lithe, supple, humanoid legs . . . and topping them off with a face only an ichthyologist could love.

Not surprisingly, sailors considered this compromised coquette to be something less than a catch, and her unnerving puckering and constant gasps for attention were enough to put off all but the most devoted leg man. Indeed, not even an admiral's share of rum was enough to steer a lonely deckhand into the scaly arms of this inverted fish fatale, and her disturbing adroitness on solid ground had even land-lubbers beating this maritime monstrosity back into the murky depths from whence she came.

By the end, entire navies of distressed seamen had hurled themselves onto the rocks rather than be carried to safety by such an unfortunate visage; it hardly bears stating that the would-be siren's swim in the dating pool was mercifully short-lived.

FEEDS ON: *Low-hanging fruit.*

HABITAT: *Treacherous rocks where she can prey on the desperate and the drowning.*

DEFENSE MECHANISMS: *Insisting there are other fishermen in the sea.*

MATING HABITS: *You don't want to know what this one would do with a drunken sailor.*

MAID-MER

UNCHAMELEON

Iguanus Nonblendicus

Few species have endeavored to stand out from the evolutionary tree quite as deliberately as this contrarian chordate, whose pathological need to distinguish himself from his surroundings included not only his questionable taste in color schemes, but his outrageous opinions and social views as well. From the spiritual emptiness of arboreal life to the overratedness of zygodactylism, every ounce of pigment seemed calibrated to flaunt conventional patterns of thinking and provoke a reaction with the most convoluted of arguments. He could expound at length about the shortcomings of prehensile tails or the merits of oviparous versus ovoviviparious reproduction, and his rant on how stereoscopic vision was part of a larger iguana conspiracy was enough to get the eyes of even the most open-minded reptile rolling in their turrets.

But if the exasperating exotherm's colorful rhetoric and reflexive owl apologism got under his fellow lizard's skin, his uncamouflaged popularity with the local garter snakes, hornbills, and coucals was hardly up for debate, and before his rapidly extrudable tongue could alienate his attackers with another tortured bit of reasoning, every predator in the sublocale was jumping on the chance for a piece of his distinctive flavor of rhetoric. The serpentine separatist was characteristically slow to see the others' points, and nowadays even the most unseasoned herpetologist would agree that his unblinking refusal to adapt was in conflict with one of the most basic tenets of Darwinian success. Though, were he still around, he'd probably beg to differ.

FEEDS ON: *Unexpected insects, counterintuitive worms.*

HABITAT: *Highly divergent branches and riverbanks.*

DEFENSE MECHANISMS: *Spotty reasoning, checkered logic.*

MATING HABITS: *Mates countercyclically, insisting that reproduction is overrated anyway.*

UNCHAMELEON

Illustration courtesy of the Museum of Failular Zoology
Copyright 2013. All rights reserved.

FAKE TITMOUSE
Rodentus Augmenticus

There was nothing modest about this mammoth-chested Minnie, who decided to get some help in the mammary department to give her a copious lift on the competition. Although serving no real biological function (in fact, they made scurrying quite an uncomfortable affair), her bodacious melons certainly made all the vermin squeak, turning whiskers whenever she would stand up to "accidentally" flash her bountiful augmentations in the name of "getting a better look around the crawlspace."

But such absurd top-heavyness wasn't always an easy load to bear. Besides the tendency to get stuck in tight crevices, all but the most pious church mouse was hard-pressed to maintain eye contact with her for more than a few seconds, and even those who did have something going on above the neckline eventually realized they would just never be taken seriously by the colony. In the end, evolution opted for a nice set of naturals, and this so-called improvement on nature ended up going bust.

FEEDS ON: *Cheese baskets sent by admirers, her power over the weaker sex.*

HABITAT: *Prefers a supportive environment.*

DEFENSE MECHANISMS: *Suggestive, low-cut fur.*

MATING HABITS: *Flaunts her body, but ultimately claims she wants to be appreciated for her mind.*

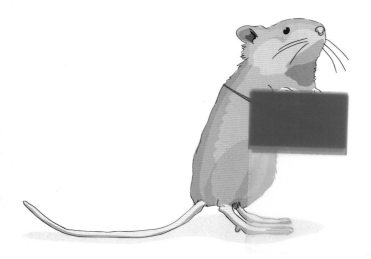

FAKE TITMOUSE

Illustration courtesy of the National Failimal Conservatory
Copyright 2013. All rights reserved.

BOOZEHOUND

Animalis Partyus

Owing to a genetic predisposition, this fun-loving mongrel's epic benders were legendary in the annals of canine history. With a nose for fermented grains, fruits, and barley, Boozehound could sniff out a good time from miles away, and once he got started, you could bet your bottom dewclaw he'd be leashing one on like it was the last days of the Miocene.

At first, early man and pack alike found his inebriated antics a howl, and the ability to track down the hooch made him a popular mutt around the camp. But by the end, his stunts began to wear thin: his constant fighting; slurred, rambling barking; and propensity to mate with whatever bitch walked into the cave alienated him from his fellow pooch. Soon his masters found him showing up increasingly late for hunts, often becoming frustrated with his trouble cantering in a straight line or his passing out in midfetch.

Finally, after one too many mornings rolling over in a puddle of his own drool and having to steady his shaky paws by consuming a little hair of himself, the carousing cur was forced to wake up, face reality muzzle-on, and admit that the party had to come to an end. Compelling evidence that man's best friend was probably not meant to also be his drinking buddy.

FEEDS ON: *Salty snacks, anything fermented.*

HABITAT: *Wherever the party is.*

DEFENSE MECHANISMS: *Aggressiveness, slurred protests of his own sobriety, breath that could kill a mastodon.*

MATING HABITS: *Hits on anything walking on four legs, though performance is hardly guaranteed.*

BOOZEHOUND

ATHEIST MANTIS

Mantis Nonbelievus

The power of prayer held little sway over this blasphemous stick bug, who made no effort to camouflage his position on the existence of a higher insect. Adhering to a strict philosophy of personal accountability, the agnostic ambush predator believed the shrubs, flowers, and katydids were all created by a set of random events, and that when you were plucked off a leaf by a passing fruit bat or had your head torn off by a female after copulation, that was simply all there was.

But while he condemned other bugs of faith for being softheaded, his nihilistic view of an impersonal universe offered little solace in times of adversity. When finally faced with the crushing emptiness that lay beyond his patch of leaf litter, the heretical hexapod could barely be bothered to eat his aphids, let alone wrap a frothy mass of eggs around a plant stem for protection against parasitic wasps. While a valid example of evolutionary principles, perhaps his own emotional chemistry could have used a little more intelligent design.

FEEDS ON: *Feeling intellectually superior.*

HABITAT: *A logical thicket in a scientific forest in a cold and deeply impersonal universe.*

DEFENSE MECHANISMS: *He doesn't need a defense mechanism. You're the one that needs a defense mechanism.*

MATING HABITS: *Open to dating those with other beliefs, but usually ends up saying something offensive.*

ATHEIST MANTIS

Illustration courtesy of the Institute of Applied Failimal Science
Copyright 2013. All rights reserved.

BIPOLAR BEAR

Moodus Erraticus

Living on the edge of the frozen sea is no day at the beach, and those long nights on the ice pack can expose cracks in the emotional state of all but the most grounded polar inhabitants. Such may have been the case for this erratic apex predator, whose unpredictable moods could drift from warm-blooded one minute to bitterly frosty the next.

He might at one point skip hibernation in a frenzied mania—frantically straightening up the ice floe while mapping out plans to move to Costa Rica and become an herbivore—only to later hole up for months in his den, depressed and emerging just to give away his collection of whale blubber and seal carcasses to some completely random arctic fox.

Whether genetic, learned, or just an excuse to be moody, his increasingly vacillating behavior confounded friends and potential mates alike, and, as living with him just made the long polar nights even longer, this hot-and-cold-running subspecies ultimately failed to gain traction on the permafrost.

FEEDS ON: *Depends on the day you ask.*

HABITAT: *The highest ice shelves, the lowest tundras.*

DEFENSE MECHANISMS: *A manic roar followed by prolonged, depressive wailing.*

MATING HABITS: *Likes to switch roles.*

BIPOLAR BEAR

FERAL POODLE
Yappus Psychoticus

Far from the lovable companions we know today, this pint-size Ghengis Khan roved the ancient jungle in packs, striking fear into the hearts of his prey with his incessant, cacophonous yelping. Shattering the peace of the forest canopy with his chilling cries for blood sacrifice and feasting as much on fear as on the disemboweled entrails of his victims, the pom-pom-headed predator more than earned his fearsome reputation as the Caligula of the Olduvai. Moreover, evidence shows that the murderous breed may have even killed for sport.

So widespread was his carnivorous orgy of violence that at one time this miniature marauder's very existence threatened to upend the natural balance of the ecosystem, until finally the larger animals were prevailed upon to stamp out this menace, forcibly pulling the fearsome ankle-biter out of the gene pool once and for all.

He was not missed much.

FEEDS ON: *Everything in his murderous path.*

HABITAT: *Caves decorated with the entrails of his victims.*

DEFENSE MECHANISMS: *The ability to tune out victims' cries for mercy.*

MATING HABITS: *Tends to do it like an animal, even by an animal's standards.*

FERAL POODLE

Illustration courtesy of the Museum of Failular Zoology
Copyright 2013. All rights reserved.

CURLYSTRAW MOSQUITO

Anopheles Ridicules

Subscribing to the theory that a two-week life span was too short not to have a little fun, this eccentric ectoparasite with an improbable proboscis briefly stirred up a buzz and thumbed its nose at the straight and narrow, keeping life in the ponds of standing water from turning stagnant. With its corkscrew series of twists and turns, his ludicrous labium initially made him something of a salt-marsh sensation, and the novelty of watching those platelets wind their way up its circuitous route certainly made the chore of bloodsucking suck a little less.

But while his meandering mouthpiece injected some levity into the Jurassic troposphere, the valuable extra seconds it took to transport T cells around all those S curves and Q bends just gave hosts more time to smack his silly face squarely into the next temperate zone. Coupled with an inconvenient tendency toward clotting, this specialized attachment turned out to be little more than a transparent gimmick, as once again nature's tendency to favor only the most pragmatic adaptations proved to be rigidly inflexible.

FEEDS ON: *The blood of really, really slow-reacting hosts.*

HABITAT: *Wacky wetlands, quixotic quagmires, goofy glades.*

MATING HABITS: *Finds it hard to enter into something with a straight face.*

DEFENSE MECHANISMS: *Being zany for the sake of being zany.*

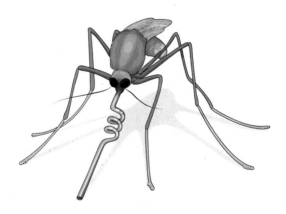

CURLYSTRAW MOSQUITO

Illustration courtesy of the Failimal Literacy Project

RASTAFARIANTELOPE

Antilocapra Stonicus

An herbivore in the truest sense of the word, this laid-back leaper wasn't afraid to buck the system, skanking across the savannah spreading his semimystical beliefs and preaching the gospel of a certain type of foliage. Not much for breeding or defending his territory, the dreadlocked impala was content to graze on his favorite weed all day long, sometimes missing entire migrations while lying in the field, braying about the oneness of all species and zoning out on the clouds above.

Needless to say, this chilled-out lifestyle wasn't ideally suited for the rigors of his surroundings. His insatiable appetite attacks would often leave the grasslands barren, and a lack of interest in sprinting left him vulnerable to hungry wildcats with a less than mellow vibe. Whether a true expression of his ideology or just an escape from the stress of the plains, the ganja-loving gazelle's habit took a toll on his motivation for survival. History suggests he may have been better off had he just laid off the grass, or at least kept his activities strictly recreational.

FEEDS ON: *Weed and whatever he's jonesing for a few hours later.*

HABITAT: *Jah Serengeti, mon.*

DEFENSE MECHANISMS: *Insisting he can cut down anytime he wants.*

MATING HABITS: *Chronically apathetic toward sex.*

RASTAFARIANTELOPE

Illustration courtesy of the Royal Failimal Society, Jamaica
Copyright 2013. All rights reserved.

REVERSE OCTOPUS

Octopoda Calamitus

The result of crossed signals higher up in the gene pool, this poor sucker developed just one good arm but eight opinionated heads to fight over it. Coining the adage "Two minds are better than one but eight is a blasphemy against God's grand design," the octo-faced oddity was constantly entangled in struggle for control of his limited resource. Decisions as simple as which camouflage to adopt would be debated for hours, and agreeing on a coconut shell to use for shelter literally took an act of congress. Problems even arose over whose turn it was to refill the ink sac, which was constantly being discharged whenever someone—usually the more cowardly cranium—perceived as an enemy something that usually turned out to be just seaweed.

The constant struggle to reach a quorum led to a plan to draw up a tentacle "share sheet" on the ocean floor, but of course, nobody could decide who would get to draw it, and by that time they had pretty much run out of ink anyway. A classic example of extinction by committee.

FEEDS ON: *Still undecided.*

HABITAT: *Still working on it.*

DEFENSE MECHANISMS: *He'll let you know.*

MATING HABITS: *TBD.*

REVERSE OCTOPUS

Illustration courtesy of the Center for Failimological Research
Copyright 2013. All rights reserved.

ELVISAURUS
Tyrannosaurus Pelvicus

When Elvisaurus burst onto the Jurassic stage with his bad-boy good looks and trademark sneer, it seemed like his immortal status on the evolutionary scene was assured. Almost overnight, young therapods were captivated by his scandalous gyrating movements and mildly anti-establishment image, not to mention a riotously catchy mating call that combined and challenged diverse influences to create a genera all his own.

Evidence shows that females were powerless against his charms, and his loner charisma usually won over his detractors as he crooned and gyrated his way to his status as King of all Reptiles. Unfortunately, this lizard legend's popularity didn't do much to boost his running speed, and once the groupies finally caught up with him, they ending up tearing him limb from limb in an orgy of estrus-crazed prehistoric lust.

While some claimed his extinction was a ruse and that he was in fact merely hiding out in some remote backwater far from the spotlight, sightings went uncorroborated, and fossil records indicate that long before his disappearance was made official, Elvisaurus had indeed left the floodplain.

FEEDS ON: *Stegasaur sandwiches, triceratops chitlins, pterodactyl wings and gravy.*

HABITAT: *On the road, usually.*

DEFENSE MECHANISMS: *Immobilizes enemies with a single hip thrust or a suggestive curl of his dangerous, pouting lips.*

MATING HABITS: *Females will give their last egg for this hunka burnin' lizard.*

ELVISAURUS

Illustration courtesy of the Museum of Failular Zoology
Copyright 2013. All rights reserved.

TRANSLUCENT KITTEN

Felis Disgusticus

Kittens are normally considered one of the most irresistible baby mammals ever to wrestle a ball of string. But those big, pleading eyes and mewling appeals for affection that worked for the common kitty failed to elicit much sympathy for this perversely pigmented prepubescent, whose off-putting lack of color where it counted provided an early evolutionary example of the phrase "too much information."

While the reason for his revealing exterior remains opaque, the impish exhibitionist's exposed inner life was too explicit for the rest of the litter to stomach, and his shockingly public intimate functions were enough to put the most devoted mother off her lunch. His carefully calculated pleas for affection only called more attention to his highly visible viscera, and ordinarily "cute" activities like curling up in a sunbeam or leaping playfully at a passing butterfly only exacerbated the unsettlingly graphic effect.

Inevitably left to fend for himself, clearer evolutionary heads stepped in, ultimately finding the see-through scamp in gross violation of the natural laws of decency. Even in an age where the need for privacy seems to be a thing of the past, it's still abundantly clear that some personal details are better left to the imagination.

FEEDS ON: *The hope that someone will actually pet it.*

HABITAT: *Out of the line of sight of the squeamish.*

MATING HABITS: *Never keeps secrets, though oversharing is often a problem.*

DEFENSE MECHANISMS: *Rubbing repulsively against a predator's leg, curling up disgustingly for its approval.*

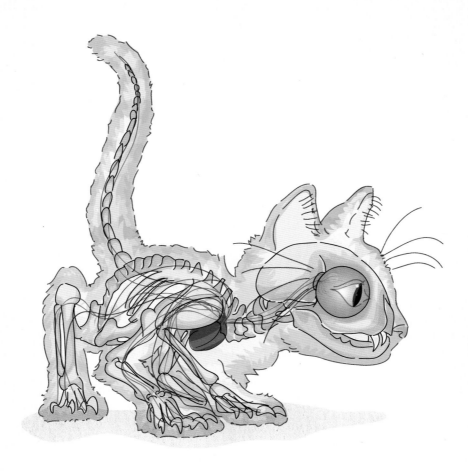

TRANSLUCENT KITTEN

Illustration courtesy of National Failimal Conservatory
Copyright 2013. All rights reserved.

MUFFINTOPOTAMUS
Hippus Unsightlius

Sometimes nature takes a turn for the tacky, as was certainly the case with this common-sense-defying river beast. Not quite fat, not quite skinny, male hippos didn't know what to make of this delusional herbivore whose hip-hugging hide bunched her belly roll in such an unflattering way as to actually call more attention to the extra pounds.

Of course, there's no shame in being full-figured in the hippo world. But even a species that spends much of its time neck deep in mud expects its kin to conduct themselves with a modicum of self-respect. In the bid to pass on her ill-fitting genes, this freshwater faux pas simply didn't do herself any favors.

FEEDS ON: *Weeds and river grasses that go straight to her hips.*

HABITAT: *Anywhere she can overexpose her generous spare tire.*

DEFENSE MECHANISMS: *Refuses to accept the limitations of her body type.*

MATING HABITS: *Attempts to lure males with off-putting wiggling, overly suggestive jiggling, and tracksuits.*

MUFFINTOPOTAMUS

Illustration courtesy of the Institute of Applied Failimal Science
Copyright 2013. All rights reserved.

MULLET MULLET

Longus Shorticus

With an unmistakable fringe that helped him swim against the tides of conformity, this hard-partying Perciform must surely have been nature's way of having its plankton and eating it too. Sporting a luxurious mane that seemed to say "business in the dorsal, party in the lateral," the bi-level bottom-feeder's moderately rebellious head-flap was as much a lifestyle choice as a signal to like-minded mates. By day, he could blend in with the school, responsibly scavenging edible mollusks and crustaceans from the benthic sediment. But when the last rays of sun departed from the depths, he would shake off the deep-sea grind to rock the reef away, or to spawn with fellow fin-bangers like it was the last mating season in the intertidal zone.

But playing by nature's rules while flaunting them at the same time just seemed to open up a can of worms. Whatever advantages his dichotomous do conveyed couldn't overcome the aesthetic compromises of such a have-it-both-ways strategy. Inevitably, schoolmates who had long since evolved and moved on were surprised to find he was still doing the same thing he had been doing since the late Cretaceous period.

In the end, partying like it was going out of style proved prophetic, and while similar aberrations can still be found in some brackish backwaters or vaguely ironic tide pools, even his friends agreed that nature's decision to give it the chop in favor of something a little more current was ultimately for the best.

FEEDS ON: *Supersize mollusks, deep-fried crustaceans, whatever he can find on a stick or in a can.*

HABITAT: *Waters with high concentrations of heavy metals.*

DEFENSE MECHANISMS: *Rocking out, partying hearty, working for the weekend.*

MATING HABITS: *Anything with gills, man.*

MULLET MULLET

FRAGRANT SKUNK
Skunkus Aromatus

For a brief, sweet-smelling time in the Oligocene forest, this marvelously scented Musteloid freshened the fenlands and spruced up the swamps with an odor so captivating no mammal with a heart and a working set of olfactory glands could resist his charms. An early trailblazer in the blossoming field of pheromones, the perfumed polecat was constantly developing new weapons in the name of sexual one-upmanship, wooing mates with a heady bouquet of aromas that included Jurassic Juniper, Pleistocene Pine, Late-Devonian Lavender, and Carboniferous Citrus Zest.

Such a potpourri of armaments was nothing to sniff at, and the four-legged lothario's penchant for releasing his intoxicating effluent when excited made him a redolent success on the mating scene. Other species began to catch wind, and soon an interspecies sensory arms race was in full bloom. Before long, every horny cougar and eligible hyenadon was shamelessly dangling the unwitting cupid over ledges or charging and swerving at the last second in hopes of scaring up a liberal dose of his ecozone-renowned love potion.

Naturally, this reputation as a woodland aphrodisiac took a toll on the frazzled nerves and exhausted scent glands of the incensed burrower, who was soon forced to take a permanent hiatus, thus ruining it for everyone and leaving us with only the obnoxious black-and-white descendants we know and hate today. This sad tale is a pungent reminder that when it comes to using chemical attractants in the name of seduction, it's always better to err on the side of restraint.

FEEDS ON: *Honeysuckle saplings, sandalwood shoots, lilac blossoms, jasmine vines.*

DEFENSE MECHANISMS: *Spraying it on even thicker.*

HABITAT: *Lives in a cloud of his own heavenly essence.*

MATING HABITS: *Capable of overpowering pretty much anything downwind.*

FRAGRANT SKUNK

PERFECT-SMILE BEAVER

Castorus Handsomus

Long respected as a linchpin in the ecosystem, few rodents have shaped the forest like beavers, those dependable carpenters that use their chisel-like incisors to thwart erosion, recharge groundwater, and create new wetland homes for other species. But this freshwater faceman seemed to be cut from different timber, with a sawed-off set of pearly whites that dazzled the riverbank and mesmerized the waterways with its bizarre symmetrical configuration.

While clearly misaligned with the objectives of the colony, this handsome disfigurement proved a convenient excuse from all that bark-breaking labor, and soon he was carving his niche in more "diplomatic" fields, lending his face to silt-breaking ceremonies, making cameos at kit birthings, and flashing his award-winning grill at pretty much every dam opening in the riparian zone.

Still, it didn't take the others long to notice this slick-pelted pretty boy wasn't exactly pulling his weight in birch stock. As the furry freeloader continued cutting his teeth on the food pile while refusing to lift a forepaw around the den, he would often swim home from a day of lounging creekside to find that underwater entrances or, indeed, the entire lodge had mysteriously moved in the middle of the night. As such, his opportunities to float through life without getting his mandibles dirty were gradually whittled down, and when early man began hunting, this semiaquatic shirker was usually the first one to be thrown under the canal. In the end, his eagerness to play his comrades for saps appeared to go against the evolutionary grain, as this marshland malingerer proved the old chestnut that good looks and intelligence aren't always symbiotic.

FEEDS ON: *The fruits of others' labors.*

HABITAT: *Lives on the back of the working mammal.*

MATING HABITS: *Prefers his mates to be career-oriented.*

DEFENSE MECHANISMS: *Hides behind that incorrigible, aspen-eating grin.*

PERFECT-SMILE BEAVER

Illustration courtesy of the National Failimal Conservatory
Copyright 2013. All rights reserved.

EXTENSION GIRAFFE
Giraffus Altudinous

Few land animals have tested nature's maximum clearance for foolhardiness as aggressively as this top-heavy tree-grazer, who rose above crippling bouts of vertigo and the gravitational pull of common sense in a quest for peak position atop the Olduvai food chain.

Refusing to put a ceiling on his vertical potential, the gangly go-getter's willingness to ratchet things up for the choicest twigs and acacia leaves no doubt raised his stature among plains-browsers, and his ability to read weather systems before they rolled in put this sky-scraping social climber over the top in the herd hierarchy.

Of course, nothing goes up forever, and it wasn't long before the sub-Saharan social climber's un-paralleled ambition began to slant his perspective. His never-ending nape made passing cud up and down a full-time job, and the mere act of rising from the watering hole could trigger a head rush of mammoth proportions. As his cranium continued its meteoric rise, terrestrial predators increasingly found him with his head in the clouds, and once it was discovered that no one was minding the store downstairs, they found it no tall order to cut this rangy ruminant down to size.

Perhaps the thin upper atmosphere had finally gone to his head, but even for a phylum known for going above and beyond, this over-extended ungulate is today viewed as a bit of a stretch.

FEEDS ON: *Soaring seedpods, vertiginous vines, death-defying date palms, elevated elms.*

HABITAT: *High above the petty earthly concerns of the Masai.*

MATING HABITS: *Stands out with females, but outgrows his relationships quickly.*

DEFENSE MECHANISMS: *Short jokes, refusing to stoop to the level of others.*

EXTENSION GIRAFFE

Illustration courtesy of the Failimal Literacy Project

LEMURACE
Lemuridae Sequinus

If the lion was king of the jungle, this flamboyant folivore surely was the queen. Showing a flair for the theatrical since he was a kit, the preening primate lit up the supercontinent with his extravagant persona and gaudy, over-the-top vocalizations. His nest was lavishly appointed and his appearance ever-changing, given his constant shedding and replacing of colorful coats, each one glitzier and more eccentric than the last.

Although he never officially came out of the canopy, his mating habits could only be categorized as ambiguous, and his apparent disinterest in reproduction limited the chance for repeat performances. But while his campy act wasn't everyone's cup of nectar, he nevertheless managed to remain defiantly fabulous right up until his final curtain call.

FEEDS ON: *Ostentatiousness, the adulation of others, thumbing his rhinarium at his critics; not much for foraging, or physical activity in general.*

HABITAT: *A lavishly appointed nest flaunting all the trappings of his rain forest success.*

DEFENSE MECHANISMS: *Can display a withering cattiness when attacked.*

MATING HABITS: *Ambiguous, but probably isn't fooling anyone.*

LEMURACE

Illustration courtesy of the Center for Failimological Research
Copyright 2013. All rights reserved.

AFRICAN RUNNING TURTLE

Tortoise Burnrubberus

Anxious to shed his image as the pokiest reptile in the pond, this turbo-powered tortoise developed a powerful set of front and back legs to propel him across the outback at breakshell speeds. Making up for eons of inertia, the trotting testudine's lightning-fast quads were ideal for grabbing the choicest earthworms, grubs, and beetles as he burned up the veld with a vengeance that left predators eating his Mesozoic dust.

But just as he was set to outdistance his sluggish counterparts in the race for evolutionary gold, the supersonic amniote got greedy.

Opting for lighter and lighter armor to shave seconds off his running time, his risky strategy backfired, and when his hungry competitors finally managed to catch up with him, the Testarossa of terrapins quickly became the Serengeti soup du jour. While his bid to pass on his chromosomes crashed and burned, many of this eukaryotic Yeager's fossil records still stand. Although his victory lap was tragically curtailed, he is nonetheless considered a pivotal species in the development of the safety standards most cartilaginous metazoans enjoy today.

FEEDS ON: *Beetles, earthworms, endorphins.*

HABITAT: *At the head of an ever-growing cloud of dust.*

DEFENSE MECHANISMS: *His blazing speed, and precious little else.*

MATING HABITS: *Mates have to continually remind him that it isn't a race.*

AFRICAN RUNNING TURTLE

Illustration courtesy of the Faildubon Society
Copyright 2013. All rights reserved.

EMO EMU
Emu Emoticus

With his painted claws and asymmetrical plumage hanging morosely over one eye as if to block out a lonely, unfeeling world, *Emu emoticus* was a picture of taloned teenage tragedy. Though capable of sprint speeds of thirty-one miles per hour over long distances, athletics didn't really fit into the androgynous beast's sensitive image and he preferred to squat for long hours in his grassy, semisheltered hollow, pecking out questionable poetry and using his inflatable neck sac to make melodramatic sounds about unrequited love and being misunderstood.

His parents chalked his brooding self-absorption up to hormonal changes, though recent discoveries indicate it's more than likely he was just using his angst-ridden facade to pick up chicks. Then again, if you were one of the only extant members remaining in a flightless winged genus of Struthioniformes, perhaps you'd feel a little misunderstood too.

FEEDS ON: *His own glamorously tragic self-image.*

HABITAT: *Usually stands just outside the flock, pretending he doesn't want to be seen.*

DEFENSE MECHANISMS: *Purity in the face of a world that hurts him.*

MATING HABITS: *Attractive to females that fall for that whole sensitive loner thing.*

EMO EMU

SPRINGYPILLAR
Lepidopterus Springius

Of all the forms of locomotion devised to propel nature's contestants forward on the race to genealogical relevance, perhaps the most loco was reserved for Springypillar, whose strange, helical body plan and patented end-over-end stride sent him wiggling and coiling across the fundament and into the pages of entomological legend. Owing to a proprietary combination of lightness and springiness, his accordion-like "walking" action made him uniquely well-adapted for descending stepped terrain. In the right conditions, the flexible forager could move at a mesmerizing clip, cascading head over heels down leafy volcanic mountains only to quickly re-form and stand quietly upright whenever danger passed nearby.

But this revolutionary adaptation was not without its kinks, and while his baffling perpetual motion confounded predators, things seemed to lose momentum once he reached the lowlands. The gentlest upward slope regularly proved to be insurmountable, and a sudden onset of inertia could leave him paralyzed for days when no one was around to give him a tip. Even as his reliance on gravity continued to reduce his habitat options, a frustrating tendency to get tangled up in his own coils often rendered him immobile and useless. Struggling to make the grade, the looping lepidopteran found himself unprepared for evolution's uphill battle, and while his pioneering frame certainly bent over backward in the name of originality, in hindsight, it becomes clear that this forward-thinking prototype never had anywhere to go but down.

FEEDS ON: *Tends to be flexible.*

HABITAT: *Generally settles in low-lying areas.*

MATING HABITS: *Walks down stairs alone or in pairs.*

DEFENSE MECHANISMS: *Hypnotizes predators with that marvelous slinkity sound.*

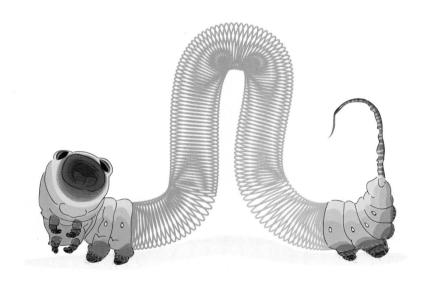

SPRINGYPILLAR

SAD CLOWNFISH

Amphipricus Tragicomicus

To the outside world, this undersea comedian was a natural cut-up, regularly filleting audiences with his dry sense of humor and fin-slapping bon mots. His hilarious water-balloon animals had the locals laughing their gills off, and a trick seaflower that squirted air always kept the tropical saltwater unexpectedly fresh.

But underneath his bubbly public persona flowed a dark undercurrent, and friends suspected his humor was a facade to keep others from truly getting close. He was prone to bouts of introspection where he would hover endlessly around the sandbar, and his brackish funks sank so deep that neither his friends nor schools of adoring damselfish could raise him from the coral bed. After a career spent turning underwater frowns upside down, one day he simply failed to resurface. Looking back, evolution would ultimately come to regard this ectothermic entertainer as a deeply conflicted and misunderstood sole, not long for this reef.

FEEDS ON: *A trove of wry observations gleaned from his lifelong status as an outsider.*

HABITAT: *Cracking the reefs up by day; haunting the sandbars at night.*

DEFENSE MECHANISMS: *Dry retorts, salty comebacks, bottomless repartee.*

MATING HABITS: *Known to seek solace in the arms of disreputable sea anemones.*

SAD CLOWNFISH

Illustration courtesy of the the Royal Failimal Society, London
Copyright 2013. All rights reserved.

NONLANDING FROG
Amphibius Splaticus

Defying gravity takes real guts, and in the end, guts were all that was left of this evolutionary Icarus, whose stratospheric hops made it nearly impossible to negotiate his inevitable reunion with the ground. Equipping himself with a powerful set of spring-loaded hindquarters, this powerful puddle-jumper's ability to push the surface-to-air envelope quickly put him leaps and bounds above predator and competition alike.

Still, despite his heightened defensive advantages, this amphibious astronaut's record-setting takeoffs set his flight path on a tragic trajectory. Even when he managed to avoid the jaws of some hungry low-flying bird, his questionable quads finally took him well beyond the point where he could successfully stick the landing, and before he could croak out another Hail Mary, he plummeted back to earth in a spectacularly messy touchdown. A clear-cut instance where Mother Nature should have looked before it leaped.

FEEDS ON: *Sonic booms, and whatever he can eat through a straw.*

HABITAT: *Divides his time between pond surfaces and the lower ionosphere.*

DEFENSE MECHANISMS: *The ability to leap predator zones in a single hop.*

MATING HABITS: *Jumps from one partner to the next, but things usually get messy in the end.*

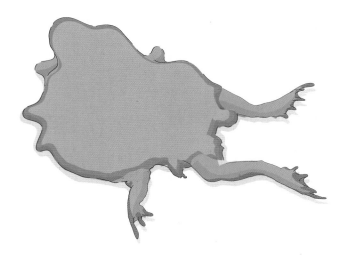

NONLANDING FROG

Illustration courtesy of the Center for Failimological Research
Copyright 2013. All rights reserved.

MARACA SNAKE

Pythonus Rhythmicus

Perhaps anticipating the eventual explosion in world music, this legless luminary traded in his trademark rattle for a less threatening, more jam-friendly instrument. Shaking his canasta-like posterior across the badlands, everywhere he slithered became an instant fiesta, and his groovy noisemaker and ear for a good beat had every coyote and kangaroo rat in the desert moving their hindquarters to his contagious Latin stylings.

A hit at mating rituals and nest-warming parties, the salsafied serpent headlined boulders, streams, and rocky outcroppings all over the substrate at the height of his popularity. However, the populace soon grew weary of the incessant up-tempo rhythms that seemed to play night and day, even, curiously, when he was nowhere to be seen.

His fickle critics finally snapped, pouncing with teeth bared and talons sharpened. It wasn't long before the party was permanently scaled back, and while there would be no more encores for this pioneering sidewinder, it remains unclear whether he was the victim of changing tastes or simply ahead of his time.

FEEDS ON: *Entrances birds and rodents, the rhythm of the night.*

HABITAT: *Session-friendly deserts and streambeds.*

DEFENSE MECHANISMS: *Grooves are thought to be highly infectious.*

MATING HABITS: *Shakes it all night long.*

MARACA SNAKE

Illustration courtesy of El Projecto de la Literatura Failimal
Copyright 2013. All rights reserved.

WHITE SUPREMACIST DOVE
Patagioenas Imbecilicus

A distant but nonetheless embarrassing familial relation of the symbols of peace we know today, this doltish dodo set himself apart from his benevolent brethren by displaying a marked intolerance for all birds of other races, creeds, and nesting instincts. Perhaps owing to inbreeding and lack of exposure to other fowl, the egg-laying xenophobe hoped to establish a pure avian race and was often seen promoting his hateful agenda by vandalizing trees that were home to "inferior" species.

Fortunately, his more famous peace-loving cousin countered his ignorance with efforts to educate and promote community outreach, prevailing upon the younger chicks in the bird community to reject the bigotry of their ancestors, and proving, as always, that understanding and tolerance begin in the nest.

FEEDS ON: *Intolerance, unfair stereotypes, revisionist biology.*

HABITAT: *Wherever fear and prejudice are allowed to roost.*

DEFENSE MECHANISMS: *Defecating on others' beliefs, laying his problems on other species.*

MATING HABITS: *Mates exclusively with his own, though sometimes harbors a secret, guilty attraction toward other phyla.*

WHITE SUPREMACIST DOVE

Illustration courtesy of the National Failimal Conservatory
Copyright 2013. All rights reserved.

GLOW BAT
Vampirus Florescus

While his fellow wingmen were content to hunt anonymously in the darkness, this megawatt mammal set his radar on a high-visibility position. With an anatomy so luminous it literally cast shadows over the competition, the one-mammal leather light show lit up the night sky with his incandescent exterior, enjoying a conspicuous hunting advantage as nearly every mosquito, gnat, and luna moth in the triforest area was irresistibly drawn to his phosphorescent fuselage.

Of course, life as a spotlight always comes with a price. The constant crush of admirers beating against his abdomen soon began to take its toll, and fellow cavemates took a dim view of this Eocene eyesore and his indiscreet lifestyle, squeaking with displeasure whenever he and his entourage flew home to interrupt a good day's sleep.

But while this neon nuisance didn't exactly receive glowing reviews from the neighbors, he certainly shined with the local population of nighthawks and bat owls, and before he could rack up too many citations for visual pollution, predators grabbed his switch and promptly called lights out on what was never considered one of evolution's brightest creations.

FEEDS ON: *Adoring dragonflies, starstruck mosquitoes, naive gnats.*

HABITAT: *Caves that tolerate high-visibility tenants.*

DEFENSE MECHANISMS: *Insisting he isn't just another flash in the pan.*

MATING HABITS: *Tends to be choosy; has difficulty finding mates who look decent in his lighting.*

GLOW BAT

ROCKPECKER

Peckus Stubbornicus

Whoever said insanity is doing the same thing over and over yet expecting different results could have been talking about this persevering Piciform who, bored with "the Man's" sources of nourishment, branched out from deciduous trunks and deadwood into more challenging environments in hopes of tapping into a fresh vein of that sweet, sweet arthropod booty. Perhaps guided by the philosophy that nothing good comes easy, the stubborn sapsucker couldn't help looking for grubs in all the wrong places, leaving no rock, slab, or promontory unhammered in his questionable attempt to excavate new quarry.

But if you can't get blood from a stone, that applies double for extracting termites, caterpillars, and beetle larvae. And so, after a hard day busting his beak in vain, the punchy pecker could very often be found staggering in circles chirping to himself, or lying petrified on the ground after flying smack into one of the same trees he tried to steer clear of in the first place. While you have to admire his granite resolve, the misguided miner never quite hit the genetic mother lode, and even though you can't accuse him of never using his noggin, it's safe to say this hard-luck headbanger was always a few minerals short of a deposit.

FEEDS ON: *An enviable sense of optimism.*

HABITAT: *Sheer limestone faces, unyielding basalt walls, impenetrable igneous rocks.*

DEFENSE MECHANISMS: *Denial, obstinacy, false hope.*

MATING HABITS: *Always wants something concrete, but in the end, it's too much of a headache.*

ROCKPECKER

SPORKBILLED PLATYPUS

Ornithorhynchus Sporkus

As far as modifications go, you'd think a webfooted, beaver-tailed, egg-laying mammal would have had enough on his genetic plate, but this peculiar offshoot decided to take it even one adaptation odder, incorporating a serrated set of equidistant prongs into his rounded, ducklike snout. Initially touted for his versatility, the cutting-edge contrivance was meant to serve as a convenient all-in-one tool, with a concave bottom that allowed the user to ladel up soil from the soupy river bottom, while triangular tines could be used to skewer whatever chunks of food came its way.

But it's tough to improve on an icon, and in attempting to perform two jobs at once, his dubious dipper failed to do either one particularly well. Those spaced-out grooves often allowed important bits of silt to slip right through, while its shallow points proved woefully inadequate for spearing bulky crustaceans. Aside from such functional compromises, its quirky hybrid shape had difficulty gaining acceptance in polite monotreme society, which considered its design idiosyncratic even for a clade of venomous knuckle-walkers that stored their fat reserves in their tails. Finding himself in breach of streambed etiquette, the Quaternary curio was soon relegated to only the most casual creekbeds, and while you have to give him credit for taking a stab at something different, this antipodean anomaly failed to find a proper placesetting at the water table.

FEEDS ON: *Creamed shellfish, mashed yabbies, laid-back subtropical fare in general.*

HABITAT: *Likely to be found in informal foraging establishments.*

MATING HABITS: *His jagged bill can be used to spear predators, but only to a point.*

DEFENSE MECHANISMS: *Mates like his versatility, but penetration usually becomes an issue.*

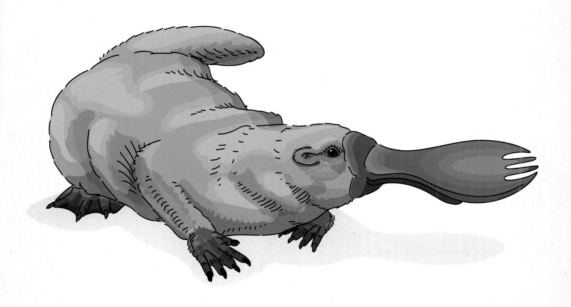

SPORKBILLED PLATYPUS

Illustration courtesy of the Faildubon Society
Copyright 2013. All rights reserved.

RE-REGENERATING LIZARD
Limbus Neverendicus

The ability to shed and replace a limb in order to shake off predators has always been one of Mother Nature's most ingenious defense mechanisms. In this case, she decided to double down on the concept, giving this prolific reptile the ability to reproduce not one but two copies of the absconded appendage.

But the Cretaceous forest was a rough place to regrow up, and it wasn't long before things started getting a little crowded for the prolific polypod, whose exponentially expanding body plan quickly became an organizational cluster-fuck.

Inevitably, the poor soul degenerated into an immobilized tangle of regenerated legs, arms, and tails. Bad for him, but good for local population, who ultimately had their pickings at what turned out to be the genetic equivalent of an all-you-can-eat limb buffet.

FEEDS ON: *The hope of a quick death.*

HABITAT: *Tries to stay mobile, but inevitably becomes rooted down over time.*

DEFENSE MECHANISMS: *Giving an arm and a leg. And an arm and a leg . . . and an arm . . .*

MATING HABITS: *Generally has his own reproductive issues to worry about.*

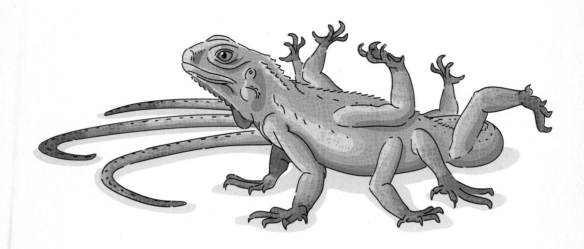

RE-REGENERATING LIZARD

Illustration courtesy of the Royal Failimal Society, London
Copyright 2013. All rights reserved.

OBESE CHEETAH
Felis Fattassicus

Like an athlete whose success goes to his stomach, things got ugly in a hurry when the former land-speed record-holder let himself go. Turning his spots on years of carb-counting and lean zebra meat in pursuit of ever more impressive velocities, the "Andretti of the Serengeti" finally decided to put some distance between himself and his training regimen. And once the pressure was off, the gluttony was on.

Content to coast off former glories, the one-time speed demon hit the wildebeests with a vengeance, tearing into family-size cuts of the biggest, slowest gnu and gazelles on the menu. Apparently lacking the chromosome for discipline, it was not uncommon to see him polishing off an entire rack of impala ribs with a double side of hyrax giblets, then washing it down with a generous portion of bushbuck gravy and perhaps a small family of guineafowl for dessert. Even his diurnal nature couldn't prevent his midnight raids on the local termite mound or perhaps a covert visit to his secret stash of springbok stuffed into a baobab tree.

Rolling down the steppes in a calorie-fueled spiral of shame, his growing waistline eventually expanded to eclipse his catlike reflexes, and it wasn't long before the only exercise he was getting was an exercise in insulin injection.

Then again, perhaps it was all just glandular.

FEEDS ON: *Whatever he can get his chubby paws around.*

HABITAT: *Wherever he can fit his fat ass.*

DEFENSE MECHANISMS: *Losing himself in a pint of antelope entrails.*

MATING HABITS: *His love of food always comes first.*

OBESE CHEETAH

Acknowledgments

For their research contributions, field expertise, and material—genetic or otherwise—we would like to thank the following: Terry and Lil Cooney, Teri Tomblin and David Adler, Veronica Vega, Jenny Holzer, Charles Darwin, Wikipedia, our heroic agent, Kathy Green, and our intrepid editor, Adam Wilson, for helping the project evolve and thrive.

Bibliography

Baker, J. (1994). *Failimals: Mother Nature's Greatest Misses*. Minutemen Press, Boston.

Bill, F. (1981). *Disgrace Under Pressure: Deep Sea Failimals*. Morrison University Press, Texas.

Brucker, B. (1991). *Fast Until They Weren't: Obese Cheetah and the African Running Turtle*. The Faildubon Society, New York.

Caputo, G. (1998). *Cretaceous Minds: Remembering Elvisaurus*. McCabe's Press, New York.

Charles, T. H. (2009). *Extinct by a Mile: Principles of Failimal Taxonomy*. Jason Street Press, London.

Cohen, R. P. (2002). *Straight to Fossil: Extreme Missteps of the Mesozoic*. A. Silva & Partners, The Hague.

Cotzias. C (1969). *Maladaptive Monotremes, Vols II & III*. Torchia, Helm & Lavery, Oxnard.

Davis, B. (1993). *Boozehounds and Bucktooth Swans: Social Behaviors of Failimals*. Smithenheim Foundation, Toronto.

Driggs, S. (1997). *Do These Genes Make Me Look Doomed to Obscurity? New Failimals of the Modern Age*. Nicollet Press, Utah.

Evanisko, M. (1975). *I, Failimal: Ecology and Habitat of the Rastafariantelope*. Robinson, Kealy & Partners, Cambridge.

Finkelstein, H. (2002). *Koalamprey and Pleather Cow: Quaternary Catastrophes*. Academic College Press, New York.

Fisher, E. M. (1978). *Rattle and Fail: An Unauthorized Biography of Bono-bo*. Cape Town Academic Press, South Africa.

Foreman, E. (1981). *Unnatural Selections (Journal of Egregious Biology)*. Edina University Press, New Orleans.

Gifford, B. (1994). *Fragrant Skunk: The Scent of Extinction*. Palmer Goodby Press, Baltimore.

Harringa, J. (2000). *Doomed by Nature: Biology, Behavior, and the Fossil Record*. American Independent Press, Boulder.

Hauen, J. R. (1993). *Badaptations: A Failimal Compendium*. Del Rey Press, Baltimore.

Hinsch, A. M. (1975). *Bunny Slipper's Ghost: Failimals Among Us*. Dulcinea University Press, New York.

Hopkins, J. B. (1968). *Tastes Like Centichicken: Failimal Predators*. Morgan University, London.

Hubbard, J. (1980). *Unchameleon: Forever Against Nature*. Erkan and Grace, Richmond.

Hurley, M. (1988). *Extinct and Extincter: Recent Studies in Failiobiology*. Olympia University Press, Philadelphia.

Hutchinson, K. (1971). *How Now, Pleather Cow? Blunders of the Bovine World*. Vail University Press, Colorado.

Krissanavich, K. (Ed) (1989). *Sistematika Failimatayuschkhick [Systematics of Failimals]*. Volstock, Moscow (in Russian).

Lescarbeau, M. (1996) *Eat, Prey, Lose: Muffintopotamus and Bipolar Bear*. Kings Head Press, Minneapolis.

Lester, G. (2001). *A Funny Thing Happened on the Way to the Pleistocene Era*. Boots & Sons, Sydney.

Lillie, A. C. (1946). *Don't Tell Darwin the Eukaryote is Dead*. Greibesland University Press, Norway.

Lundberg, S. (2000). *The Rise and Fall of Extension Giraffe*. Sidewalk Press, England.

Lupinacci, T. (1985). *Failimal Insects: Flies in the Primordial Soup*. The Museum of Irregular Zoology, England.

Mahoney, S. (1982). *Facedown in the Gene Pool*. Van Graves Reinbold, Chicago.

Mann, J. (1975). *Failwissenschaften*. Schnoor, Germany.

Marucci, J. (1979). *Instinct or Idiocy? Failimal Psychology*. Merkin & Woolcott Publishers, New York.

McCann, J. (1986). *Dieting Strategies of the Waif Walrus*. Bullet Press, Glasgow.

McHugh, P. (ed) (1998). *New American Failmanac*. Kings Head Press, Minneapolis.

McKay, K. (1990). *It Seemed like a Good Idea at the Epoch*. Bruin University Press, Virginia.

Morrison, J. (1981). *DNA-Holes: Genetic Anomalies in the Wild*. Berrigan & Co., Oxford.

Naylor, N. (2004). *Combover Eagle: History and Biology of a Solitary Species*. Vinnoir Press, England.

Owens, A. R. (1999). *A Natural History of Hibernating Glow Bats*. Oxnard University Press, Boston.

Richards, I. L. (1976). *Chromaso-so at Best: The Genealogy of Failure*. Eisner Museum of Natural History, New South Wales.

Ruth, I. F. (1975). *Lemurace and the Dawn of the Sequined Age*. Webber University Press, Ithaca.

Sheahan, M. (1996). *Our Failimals, Ourselves*. Witherspoon Press, San Francisco.

Silver, E. (1995). *Burnt Umberjay: The Color of Futility*. Blaylock, Bekesz, and Associates, New South Wales.

Simon, F. (ed.) (1993). *Evolosers: Darwin's Lament*. Brindfors University Press, Stockholm.

Terrence, E. C. (1946). *The Paleocene Error: An Ecological Thriller*. Jameson Press, Roscommon.

Thomas, C. (1982). *Evolution of the Maraca Snake: One Slither Forward, Two Slithers Back*. Mizzen Publishers, New Delhi.

Thompson, L. (1980). *Dead by Design: Failimals of Western Australia, Vols I & II*. Melbourne Zoological Society, Australia.

Tso, C. (2000). *Nowhere to Go but Down: Failimal Burrowers*. Silver & Partners, Bangkok.

Vaughan, E. (2012). *50 Shades of Fail: The Sex Lives of Failimals*. Shakti University Press, New York.

Vega, V. P. (2010). *Jurassic Jerks and the Triceratops Who Loved Them*. Shakti University Press, New York.

Weiss, A. (1979). *Of Chauvinist Pigs and Fake Titmice: Reproductive Politics of Failimals*. The Museum of Irregular Zoology, England.

Zimner, J. (ed) (2007). *One-Hatch Wonders: The North American Failimal Registry, Vol II*. Shore Acres Press, Chicago.